D1484033

Go BiG!

By Joyce L. Rodgers

Go BiG!

By Joyce L. Rodgers

NUVISION PUBLISHING

Scriptures are taken from The Holy Bible
King James Version
(Public Domain)

Books may be ordered through booksellers
or by contacting:
www.joycerodgers.org

First Printing: 2017

ISBN 978-0-578-19652-7

Cover design by
DeShon Gales for DG Creative Studio

Art Direction by Christopher Coleman,
I Think For You Consulting, LLC

NuVision Publishing
PO Box 4455 | Wilmington, NC 28406
www.nuvisiondesigns.biz/publishing

Printed in the United States of America.

Dedication

I dedicate this book to all of you who have a desire to do big things in life. As you absorb the content on each page, I pray that you are infused with the courage to step out and go after Everything God has for you.

Thank you for taking a leap of faith.

Acknowledgements

Thank you, Jesus for counting me worthy to represent you in the earth and placing me in the ministry. You have been with me every step of the way. To my loving mother, "Ma Dear," thank you for your lifetime of love and prayers. (Mom, heaven is blessed to have you.) To my wonderful brothers, sisters, nephews and nieces, there are no words to express my love and appreciation for you. To my dynamic church leaders, church families, friends, and ministry team, your touch has caused such growth in my life. Lastly, **thank you Jesus**! I know I thanked you already, but I want those who read this to know that everything starts with you and everything ends with you. Without you there is no me. I love you forever!

Table of Contents

Introduction
It's Time to GO BiG

Are you guilty of small-minded thinking? From either a natural or spiritual standpoint, do you tend to be timid and afraid to put yourself out there because it's too risky? Do you default to your comfort zone due to fear of things not working out in the end for you? Are you so afraid of failure that you won't even try?

That's exactly what happened in the book of Numbers, chapter 13, when the twelve spies approached the Promised Land to scout out what it had to offer. After looking around they could not deny that it was truly a land flowing with milk and honey, just as God had said, and had every good thing in great abundance, including gigantic grape clusters and incredibly fertile black soil. Then they saw the giants, the sons of Anak, and they became paralyzed with fear and dread. Except for Joshua and Caleb, the rest of the spies were struck with terror. They saw themselves as grasshoppers and made an informed decision to not believe what God had said -- that they were to take the land and make it their own, because He had already decreed it was so. They scurried to retreat and never even tried to do what God commanded.

As I travel the length and breadth of America and the world, I am stunned to find that so many people function under a "grasshopper" mindset; everything and everyone looks larger than life compared to what they see when they look at themselves. As a result, they believe they are powerless. Others are like Peter and some of the disciples who spent their time toiling away, with little-to-show for their labor (Luke 5:6). They live their lives fishing too close to the bank, if you will, and constantly end up frustrated and disappointed with the outcome. Many feel the need to play it safe and are too afraid to step out to see what God will do in response to their faith. Perhaps this behavior exists because they are unaware of how the Bible identifies who they are in Christ or maybe it's just their decision to walk in unbelief.

The good news is that we do not have to live with a grasshopper mentality. We don't have to settle for the status quo because God wants us to be victorious in all we set our hands to do. In fact, God desires that we take authority over the root cause of fear and timidity, the devil, because the Spirit of God lives in us, and He has already defeated our foe. We need to simply stand in agreement with what God has already done and live our lives fearlessly!

One day after Jesus finished teaching to a crowd, He told Peter to "launch out into the deep" to supernaturally pull in a massive haul of fish. When Peter did as He said the nets broke under the weight of the catch of fish. The profound truth is that you and I can do the very same thing! Friend, I'm here to tell you that it's time to push away from the bank and shake off the timidity. It's time to silence the fear, doubt and unbelief that plague us and choose to be bold and confident in the strength of the Lord, believing and living out His promises to us. It's time to GO BiG!

When you "GO BiG" it means you stop engaging in negative self-talk and behaviors and instead go after everything God has for you. In this book, I share practical examples of people in the Bible who decided to launch out and GO BiG, specifically in the areas of life, love and leadership.

I encourage you to take the time to look up the scripture references provided, to further solidify God's word in your heart and make the chapters come alive. Each chapter closes with a thought-provoking question designed to help you address the areas that may be holding you back. My prayer is that after you read this book you'll discover that you too have the capacity to Go BiG just like persons in the stories you are about to read. GOING BiG is not only a game changer-it's a life changer!

Let's GO BiG!

GO BiG In LIFE!
GO BiG – Assured of God's Protection

And ye shall hear of wars and rumours of wars: see that ye be not troubled: for all these things must come to pass, but the end is not yet.

Matthew 24:6

We live in a world filled with violence. News abounds regarding the blatant brutality of domestic hate groups and international terrorist groups. In the United States, mass shootings have almost become the order of the day. Crimes once considered inhumane now seem commonplace in comparison, so seeing them unfold no longer surprises us. Murder, rape, robbery, kidnapping, the exploitation of women and children through child pornography and human trafficking are among the long list of crimes. We live under constant threat of nuclear attack, and the notion of "peace" among world superpowers hangs by a thread. Were it not for the Lord's imminent return, man would surely self-destruct and annihilate himself.

In the book of Joshua, chapter 2, we see that Rahab and her family faced annihilation from a different source. She had heard of the God of Israel and how He had brought to his knees the once mighty and invincible Pharaoh of Egypt. Because of his disobedience to God's command to let His people go free from slavery, Egypt had been stripped bare – vegetation destroyed by locusts and other plagues, every firstborn dead, and in the end Pharaoh's army was drowned in the Red Sea. Who were these Israelites, and more importantly, who was their God? With that kind of power, surely, He reigned supreme. After facing such

GO BiG In LIFE!
GO BiG – Assured of God's Protection

profound consequences how could anyone NOT believe in Him and serve Him alone?

With those thoughts running through her mind and Jericho on lockdown by the order of the king, imagine Rahab's surprise when two men of Israel came to her door under cover of night! When they asked for shelter and wanted to know if she would hide them, Rahab was faced with a dilemma and a choice: hide the men of Israel and side with their God, or give her allegiance to the King of Jericho and sound the alarm.

A Date with Destiny

It's not clear whether Rahab knew it at the time, but both her natural and eternal destiny rested on the choice she would make that night. The circumstances of life often bring us to a literal crossroads, the outcome of which will change the very trajectory of our lives and that of our families. Rahab could have cast her lot with what was familiar, namely, the people of her country and the many gods they served. She could have chosen to stay as she was and stay where she was – or choose to cleave to the God of Israel and GO BiG.

Leaving the safety and insulation afforded by what is familiar and comfortable is not only difficult, but it can be downright terrifying. Oftentimes when faced with life-changing decisions, they are "now or never" and "do or die" moments. Rahab's interaction with the king is a perfect illustration of this reality. She had to make a decision, and she had to make it fast. When the king was informed that the spies had entered the country, he immediately sent word to Rahab, demanding that she turn over the

GO BiG In LIFE!
GO BiG – Assured of God's Protection

spies. After hiding the spies, she admitted to the messengers that she had seen the men from Israel – and then proceeded to send them on a wild goose chase to find them!

Go BIGGER

Rahab's decision to GO BiG didn't stop with hiding the spies. Yes, she had hidden the spies and decoyed the king's men, but she wanted and needed more. Her decision to go with God wouldn't just affect her life alone; it would also have a profound effect on her family, so she had to make sure that they would be protected in the process. **Going BiG doesn't just impact you; the benefits and blessings will extend to your children and your children's children.**

Having chosen to follow the God of Israel, Rahab struck a deal with the spies to see them safely out of the city if they would promise to protect her and her family. In gratitude for her help, the spies promised Rahab and her household that they would be spared from death when the Israeli army returned (Joshua 2:9-14). The agreement was made and the conditions were set (Rahab had to tie a red cord in the window that the spies would use to climb down the exterior wall of the city). And because she kept her word to protect them, Rahab and her family were saved when Jericho was destroyed.

Go Deeper

In what areas of your life do you feel vulnerable and unprotected? What steps will you take today to GO BiG, assured of the Lord's divine protection?

NOTES

GO BiG –Your Territory Is Enlarged!

And Jabez called on the God of Israel, saying,
"Oh that Thou wouldest bless me indeed, and enlarge my coast,
and that Thine hand might be with me, and that Thou wouldest
keep me from evil, that it may not grieve me!"
And God granted him that which he requested.

1 Chronicles 4:10

The prayer of Jabez is one of the shortest prayers in the Bible, yet it's also one of the most powerful. I don't know of any faithful church-goer who hasn't heard a message on blessings and prosperity. God's word literally abounds with such promises, and in the New Testament the Lord Jesus assures us that all things are possible to those who believe (Mark 9:23). And yet, if we're anything like Jabez, we're compelled to think and to pray, "Oh Lord, if you would bless me indeed – if you would truly bless me!" Jabez decided to GO BiG, and called on God to bless the four major areas of his life.

Bless Me

If you look up the word 'blessing' in the dictionary you'll see that it encompasses receiving or bestowing favor, mercy, grace, divine will, benefit, approval and a host of other things--in this case, from God. And who doesn't want that? Jabez was careful to ask God to bless him. He called on the God of Israel, looking to Him as his source. James 1:17 tells us that "Every good gift and every perfect gift is from above, and cometh down from the Father."

Oftentimes, many of us fail to pray with fervency until times of trouble. Jabez didn't wait until times got tough before seeking God in fervent prayer. He maintained his posture in prayer, taking

19

GO BiG –Your Territory Is Enlarged!

advantage of the privilege to intensively communicate with God and not withholding his request for blessing. No area of Jabez's life was too big or too small to take to God. Not a single stone was left unturned in prayer. Going BiG means believing God to bless every area of our lives-- from top-to-bottom, side-to-side; every corner, crack and crevice! It is believing God to bless always, regardless of where life takes us.

Enlarge My Territory

Jabez didn't stop with asking God to bless him; he also asked the Lord to "enlarge his coasts." In modern terms, it means Jabez asked God to enlarge his territory. Though this request included his property, he wasn't simply asking for more land. He also wanted increased responsibility. He wanted God to use him to a far greater degree. Simply put, Jabez was saying, Bring it on, Lord! I want to GO BiG for You!

Be with Me

Has the "GO BiG" aspect of Jabez's prayer hit home with you yet? Have you grasped the depth of his request—what it really means? Jabez moved from asking God to bless him and enlarge his territory to asking God for His presence. He prayed, "Be with me." Be with me, Lord, everywhere I go. In good times and bad; during my highs and lows; when I'm on track and when I'm struggling, Lord, be with me.

There is something special about walking in confidence, knowing the Lord is with you. You move forward with assurance, knowing your steps are ordered by the Lord (Proverbs 3:6). There

GO BiG –Your Territory Is Enlarged!

is no hesitation when it's time to act, and you're certainly not tentative when you move forward. When you approach life with that kind of confidence, certain that you're walking in step with the Creator of the universe, everything around you changes. Doors begin to open, and you walk in divine favor as He opens the way before you.

Keep Me from Evil and Harm

With the request to be kept from evil and harm his prayer comes full circle. He asked for (and received) God's blessing; enjoyed the enlarging of his territory and could rest, securely in the presence of the Lord. Finally, he asked the Lord to keep him from evil inside and out. Blessed from top to bottom, inside and out, Jabez was then able to GO BiG because his life was covered; going from a black and white existence to one in 3-D and living color, where nothing is impossible anymore.

Go Deeper

Which of the four components of Jabez's prayer addresses your area of greatest need? Pray the prayer of Jabez daily, focusing on that specific area. Put your faith in action and watch God work!

NOTES

GO BiG –
Prepare to Receive God's Abundance!

Now when he had left speaking, he said unto Simon,
Launch out into the deep, and let down your nets for a draught.
And Simon answering said unto him, Master,
we have toiled all the night, and have taken nothing
nevertheless, at thy word I will let down the net.
And when they had done this,
they enclosed a great multitude of fishes: and their net brake.
And they beckoned unto their partners, which were in the other
ship, that they should come and help them. And they came, and
filled both the ships, so that they began to sink.

Luke 5:4-7

How would you like to receive a boat-sinking blessing? I mean a blessing so huge that it literally sinks your boat? That's what Simon Peter and his fishing partners experienced when they <u>stopped toiling</u> and <u>started trusting</u>.

Toiling vs. Trusting

When we try to make things happen in our own strength we end up toiling. A lot of times we say we believe God, but do not. Think of three aspects of your life in which you say you believe God.

- Are you fretting?
- Doubting?
- Feeling insecure?
- Are you plagued with thoughts of, "What if God doesn't do it?"
- Have you come up with "Plan B" just in case?

GO BiG –
Prepare to Receive God's Abundance!

If you are doing any of these things, my friend, you're toiling instead of trusting. One who truly believes God makes his request in faith and trusts God for the right outcome. Doing this allows the peace of God, which passes all understanding, to keep our hearts and minds through Christ Jesus (Philippians 4:7).

Don't Rely on Your Own Knowledge

Peter and the other disciples had worked all night hoping for a great haul of fish. They needed the blessing of a big catch, yet for all their toiling, they pulled up empty nets. As experienced fisherman, they relied on their knowledge of fishing to achieve success instead of relying on God.

And you know what? I get that sometimes, because we are skilled or gifted in certain areas, we believe we "know" what we are doing and don't ask help. Look at Peter; he didn't think the presence of the Lord was necessary to pull in a great haul. Peter made his living as a fisherman and probably felt he could fish in his sleep.

Like Peter, we can choose to rely on our knowledge instead of relying on God. We depend on our life experiences, education, money, employment or connections to get us where we want to go, and turn to God in despair only when we face disappointment. Our Lord is so gracious! When we finally decide to really trust Him, He moves us into place to GO BiG.

GO BiG –
Prepare to Receive God's Abundance!

Get in Proper Position and Launch Out!

Getting into place to be blessed involves a shift in mindset. It means we set aside our own thoughts and ways of getting things done, and instead rely on the leading of the Holy Spirit--even if it takes more time than we imagined. It means first opening our minds to receive God's direction, confident that He will show us the way. It means recognizing the futility of human effort and choosing to avail ourselves of supernatural empowerment. It means pushing off from the shore, leaving our comfort zones and choosing instead to GO BiG!

"Launch out into the deep," Jesus says,
"and let down your nets for a draught."
Luke 5:4

Just as a quarterback calls the plays to get players into position, the Holy Spirit enables us to receive the direction we need when we get our minds in tune with God's will. Once that mindset shift takes place, our faith can snap into gear and move us down the field to victory. At that point, we can do exactly what Peter did and receive the epitome of abundance: a boat-sinking blessing!

Go Deeper

In what areas of your life are you toiling instead of trusting? In what areas do you allow your earthly knowledge to overrule your faith? What mindset shift needs to take place for you to get into position to GO BiG and receive God's abundance?

NOTES

GO BiG – Receive Your Physical Healing

And a certain woman, which had an issue of blood twelve years,
And had suffered many things of many physicians, and had spent
all that she had, and was nothing bettered, but rather grew worse,
When she had heard of Jesus,
came in the press behind and touched his garment.
For she said, If I may touch but his clothes, I shall be whole.
And straightway the fountain of her blood was dried up;
and she felt in her body that she was healed of that plague.
Luke 5:4-7

Those of us who regularly attend church have likely heard the story of the woman with the issue of blood. We've read the passage, heard numerous sermons preached about her and believe we know her story. When we consider reasons to "GO BiG," very few are more crucial than when we seek God for physical healing for ourselves or a loved one.

And yet, would you agree with me that in many cases we find it easier to believe God for others than we do for ourselves? When someone else is sick and in need of healing, we aren't experiencing the symptoms; we haven't received the frightening test results; we aren't taking the devastating treatments. We look to God with confidence, recognizing that "the prayer of faith shall save the sick, and the Lord shall raise him up; and if he has committed sins, they shall be forgiven him" (James 5:15). We can quote all the scriptures, share them with the sick, and trust that God will hear us and answer our prayers. But what happens when the sick person is you or me?

GO BiG – Receive Your Physical Healing

GO BiG – Or Die

Sometimes we have no other option but to GO BiG. We all encounter times in our lives when we are faced with "do or die" situations. Trying one solution and then another, we go from one extreme to the next until we have exhausted every possibility. Having reached the end of her financial rope, the woman with the issue of blood was truly out of options. She had reached the point where she had to GO BiG or die.

Expressing BiG Faith in an Unlikely Way

What I love about this woman is the fact that not only did she recognize Jesus as her one and only last resort, she moved quickly and decisively to put her healing plan into action. She knew Jesus had the power. She knew the remedy for her situation was in Him, and she knew all she had to do was touch His clothes.

Her faith was so great that she felt she had no other option than to place her life and future on the line, believing she was in Jesus' capable hands. This woman was going so BiG that she saw no need to explain or even to ask for healing.

The woman with the issue of blood teaches us that we can express BiG faith in unlikely ways. Sometimes we aren't able to have pastors anoint us with oil and pray the prayer of faith over us. Sometimes we're unable to get to church, hear a message or go to the altar. Don't allow yourself to be hindered by conventional practices and traditions. There are times we must use what we have and make do with where we are-and this woman shows us that "making do" is more than enough!

GO BiG – Receive Your Physical Healing

Right then and there, in the middle of that massive crowd, she literally seized the moment, and touched Jesus' clothes. Her faith was rewarded, and "straightway the fountain of her blood was dried up; and she felt in her body that she was healed of that plague" (Mark 5:29).

Go Deeper

Do you have a physical need that fits under the category of "do or die?" If necessary, employ some out-of-the-box thinking to receive your miracle!

NOTES

GO BiG – Deliverance Is Yours!

*And when he was come out of the ship, immediately there met him
out of the tombs a man with an unclean spirit. Who had his
dwelling among the tombs; and no man could bind him, no, not
with chains: Because that he had been often bound with fetters and
chains, and the chains had been plucked asunder by him, and the
fetters broken in pieces: neither could any man tame him.
And always, night and day, he was in the mountains, and in the
tombs, crying, and cutting himself with stones. But when he saw
Jesus afar off, he ran and worshipped him, And cried with a loud
voice, and said, what have I to do with thee, Jesus, thou Son of the
most high God? I adjure thee by God, that thou torment me not.
For he said unto him, Come out of the man, thou unclean spirit.
And they came to Jesus, and see him that was possessed with the
devil, and had the legion, sitting, and clothed,
and in his right mind: and they were afraid.*

Mark 5:2-8, 15

Demon possession is a real and deadly phenomenon. The New
Testament includes a number of examples of people bound by the
grip of the devil. Locked in the prison of possession and unable to
help themselves, they were "grievously vexed" (Matthew 15:22).
Since such incidents have been recorded it has manifested in a vast
number of symptoms, including muteness, violent seizures,
throwing victims into fire or water (Mark 9:17-22), and spirits of
infirmity that caused people to be bowed over and unable to
straighten themselves upright (Luke 13:11). Satan has carried out
his agenda using various means.

GO BiG – Deliverance Is Yours!

Running to Jesus

Jesus' stop into the country of the Gadarenes caused an immediate reaction. The demon-possessed man who lived in the cemetery ran to Jesus when he saw Him in the distance (Mark 5:6). The man was known far and wide, not only for living in the cemetery, but for continually wailing and cutting himself with stones. And try as they might, the townspeople were unable to keep him bound with chains and could not calm him down.

When the man reached Jesus, he fell to his feet and made a big show of worshipping Him. Haven't we seen demon-possessed people engaging in similar behavior in church? Their ostentatious expressions of worship are not in sync with the true flow of the Spirit. Instead, they often cause distractions by drowning out the sincere praise of those standing nearby, and their bodily contortions often become unseemly, sensual expressions. When you encounter this in a worship service, don't become alarmed. Like the demoniac, they are running to Jesus. Believe it or not, church is exactly where these individuals need to be, because the saints can GO BiG and cast the devil out!

A Legion of Devils

When we study this scene in Mark Chapter 5 we find that the man in the tombs was possessed by a legion of devils. A legion is defined as a number somewhere between 3,000 and 6,000 evil spirits. That a human being could even host such a large number of demon spirits is almost incomprehensible. But thanks be to God, nothing is too hard for the Lord! (Jeremiah 32:27) Indeed, Jesus

GO BiG – Deliverance Is Yours!

reassures us in Matthew 19:26 that with men things are impossible, but "with God all things are possible."

A Legion of Angels

If someone you love is demon-possessed, don't despair! Yes, the man in the tombs was possessed with a legion of devils, but because we belong to Christ, we have legions of angels at our disposal! When the king of Syria sent a large army to capture the prophet Elisha, his servant Gehazi was terrified by the stunning sight of horses and chariots as far as the eye could see. But because he was seasoned in the ways of God, Elisha didn't bat an eye. Instead, he turned to God and said, "LORD, I pray thee, open his eyes, that he may see" (2 Kings 6:17). The LORD opened Gehazi's eyes, and when he looked up, he could see the angelic army coming against the king's armed forces: "The mountain was full of horses and chariots of fire round about Elisha."

In 2 Kings 19:35, the angel of the Lord went out during the night and killed 185,000 Assyrian soldiers. When those who remained got up the next morning, they were surrounded by dead bodies. We have no reason to fear a legion of devils – through Jesus we have access to more than twelve legions of angels (Matthew 26:53)!

We Have the Power

If someone you love is suffering from demonic possession, take heart. Greater is He that is in us than he who is in the world (1 John 4:4)! If you're suffering from the oppression of the enemy, don't fear. Claim and stand on this promise from the Lord contained in Luke 10:19: Behold, I give unto you power to tread on serpents and scorpions, and over all the power of the enemy:

GO BiG – Deliverance Is Yours!

and nothing shall by any means hurt you. If you need to add fasting to your prayers in order to see certain strongholds destroyed and demons cast out (Mark 9:29), be willing to make the sacrifice. Remember, we have the power, and we have the Savior! GO BiG, assured of promised deliverance!

Go Deeper

What strongholds in your life (or in the lives of those you love) need to be cast down? What steps will you take today to bring about deliverance?

NOTES

GO BiG –
You Don't Have to See It to Believe It

And when Jesus was entered into Capernaum,
there came unto him a centurion, beseeching him,
And saying, Lord, my servant lieth at home
sick of the palsy, grievously tormented.
And Jesus saith unto him, I will come and heal him
The centurion answered and said, Lord, I am not worthy that thou
shouldest come under my roof: but speak the word only, and my
servant shall be healed. For I am a man under authority, having
soldiers under me: and I say to this man, Go, and he goeth; and to
another, Come, and he cometh; and to my servant, Do this, and he
doeth it. When Jesus heard it, he marvelled,
and said to them that followed, Verily I say unto you,
I have not found so great faith, no, not in Israel.
And Jesus said unto the centurion, Go thy way;
and as thou hast believed, so be it done unto thee.
And his servant was healed in the selfsame hour.
Matthew 8:5-10, 13

From a natural standpoint, the senses of sight, smell, hearing, taste and touch are very important. Sure, we can navigate without one or more of our senses, and millions of people who lack one or more senses still live fulfilling lives. Interestingly enough, some of them outshine those who have all five because they become skilled in adapting and leveraging the remaining senses to their advantage. In that case those without sight don't have to "see it to believe it," because their sense of touch is either unusually acute, or their sense of hearing is honed to a fine point. Imagine how easy it would be to GO BiG if our faith wasn't so dependent on our sense of physical sight?

GO BiG –
You Don't Have to See It to Believe It

Recognizing True Authority

The Roman centurion didn't allow his sight to block his faith. Because he recognized Jesus' authority, he didn't have to see his servant be healed to believe it would happen. Authority encompasses the intrinsic power or right to give orders to subordinates. An individual with authority is empowered to make decisions and has the ability to make things happen. The centurion, who possessed authority granted by Rome, knew the power behind his position. He was experienced in exerting his authority over his soldiers and understood that verbal commands weren't always necessary; orders were carried out with a mere flick of his wrist or a nod of his head. Keenly aware of the authority he wielded on a daily basis, he was easily able to recognize – even sense – the authority Jesus possessed.

A Divine Correlation

The centurion saw Jesus in action, healing the sick, casting out devils and opening blind eyes. In a world where people were at the mercy of their illnesses and afflictions, here was someone able to overrule disease with a command, or with the laying on of His hands. When Jesus spoke, the illnesses, diseases, afflictions and demon spirits responded and obeyed His commands. Here was true authority in action!

The centurion made the divine correlation between the exercise of authority in the natural realm and the operation of authority in the spiritual realm. Jesus' power to heal was based on His divine authority. After he asked Jesus to heal his servant, he recognized

GO BiG –
You Don't Have to See It to Believe It

Jesus' divine authority and said he wasn't worthy for Jesus to come under his roof. The correlation he made between the exercise of authority in the natural and spiritual realms enabled him to GO BiG in his request: "Speak the word only, and my servant shall be healed" (Matthew 5:8).

I Know How This Works

The centurion continued, "For I am a man under authority, having soldiers under me: and I say to this man, Go, and he goeth; and to another, Come, and he cometh; and to my servant, Do this, and he doeth it" (v. 9). In other words, "I know how this authority thing works; I use it myself. I don't have to see you heal my servant; I know all you have to do is speak and my servant will be healed."

The centurion's grasp of the divine principle of authority – and his willingness to GO BiG and use it – caused Jesus to marvel in astonishment. To some Jews he was considered a heathen, and yet this heathen's grasp of divine authority moved him leaps and bounds over those who called Abraham their "father!" Unlike the unbelieving Jews, the centurion didn't have to see it to believe it, and for that reason, was able to receive what he asked of the Lord.

Go Deeper

Do you understand how faith works hand in hand with the divine principles of authority? Do you recognize Jesus' authority over the challenges you face? Are you aware that your ability to grasp such principles enables you to Go BiG?

NOTES

GO BiG --Bring Someone to Jesus!

*And again he entered into Capernaum, after some days; and it was
noised that he was in the house. And straightway many were
gathered together, insomuch that there was no room to receive
them, no, not so much as about the door: and he preached the
word unto them. And they come unto him, bringing one sick of the
palsy, which was borne of four. And when they could not come
nigh unto him for the press, they uncovered the roof where he was:
and when they had broken it up, they let down the bed wherein the
sick of the palsy lay. When Jesus saw their faith, he said unto the
sick of the palsy, Son, thy sins be forgiven thee.*

Mark 2:1-5

We've all been there. Your dearest friend is in crisis mode,
phoning at 3 a.m. and waking you out of a sound sleep. Maybe she
just had a horrible fight with her husband and had to flee her home
because she feared for her life. Maybe he's stranded on the side of
the highway, in the middle of nowhere, with a flat tire and no
spare. Maybe she's just left the doctor's office and was told she
has a terminal illness. Quite possibly, a parent, sibling or child
passed away or was tragically killed. Regardless of the nature of
the trouble or affliction, YOU are the friend who says, "Lean on
me."

Ride or Die

The Internet is filled with memes and posts about good friends.
The expression "ride or die" is a term used to describe the type of
friend who will go with you to the end of the earth and back, with
no thought of personal cost or fear of danger. It's a combination of
the phrases "ride it out" and "die trying." Ride or die friends are

GO BiG --Bring Someone to Jesus!

the ones who see what you need and will do whatever it takes to get you where you need to go or bring you what you need.

If you're a ride or die friend, you take friendship quite seriously. With you, the words "lean on me" are not just flowery words; they're viable and meaningful. You are the friend who's willing to leave your comfort zone to render aid. You're there with a listening ear, a shoulder to cry on and a hand to hold. You're the friend who offers the spare bedroom or sofa, or presses money into a hand or pays a bill. You spring into action and you make things happen.

Bearing the Burden

The four friends in Mark 2 were the ultimate "ride or die" friends. They didn't just go the extra mile; they went above and beyond, taking the phrase "lean on me" to an entirely different level. They personified the admonition contained in Galatians 6:2, which instructs us to "Bear ye one another's burdens." These four men literally bore the burden of their paralyzed friend and did what it took to bring him to Jesus. Knowing their friend needed healing wasn't enough – they decided to do something about it.

We'll Take You There

Oh, to have friends like these! They refused to accept the status quo and wanted their friend to be healed. Hearing that Jesus was preaching and teaching in a house in Capernaum, they had to come into agreement and make a decision to GO BiG on behalf of their sick friend so he could receive the healing he so desperately

GO BiG --Bring Someone to Jesus!

needed. They had to tell him, "Jesus is in town, and we know He can heal you. We'll take you there."

Upon their arrival, they saw that the house was packed with people. Undeterred, they recognized that in this instance, to GO BiG would mean going beyond affirming Jesus' power to heal. Going BiG meant being willing to not only shake things up, but tear things up!

Take Off the Roof

Can't get through the door? Then create another entrance! Tossing caution and decorum to the winds, the four friends literally took the tiles off the roof in order to let down the bed carrying their friend – right in front of Jesus. Talk about ride or die! When Jesus saw the friends' faith, he forgave the sins of the man who was sick and made him whole. Thank God for ride or die friends who aren't afraid to GO BiG!

Go Deeper

For which friend or family member do you need to GO BiG? Do you have the audacity – and the creativity – to get that person to Jesus?

NOTES

GO BiG--Believe God for Debt Cancellation!

Now there cried a certain woman of the wives
of the sons of the prophets unto Elisha, saying,
Thy servant my husband is dead; and thou knowest that thy servant
did fear the LORD: and the creditor is come to take unto him my
two sons to be bondmen. And Elisha said unto her, What shall I do
for thee? tell me, what hast thou in the house? And she said, thine
handmaid hath not any thing in the house, save a pot of oil. Then
he said, Go, borrow thee vessels abroad of all thy neighbours, even
empty vessels; borrow not a few. And when thou art come in, thou
shalt shut the door upon thee and upon thy sons, and shalt pour out
into all those vessels, and thou shalt set aside that which is full. So
she went from him, and shut the door upon her and upon her sons,
who brought the vessels to her; and she poured out. And it came to
pass, when the vessels were full, that she said unto her son, Bring
me yet a vessel. And he said unto her, There is not a vessel more.
And the oil stayed. Then she came and told the man of God.
And he said, Go, sell the oil, and pay thy debt,
and live thou and thy children of the rest.

2 Kings 4:1-7

I don't know anyone (me included) who at some point in life hasn't been plagued by debt. According to the government's TreasuryDirect.gov website, today's Federal Debt is about $18,658,332,270,181.33 – which comes out to more than $55,621 per person. And you know what? The amount is the gross outstanding federal debt issued by the United States Department of the Treasury since 1790. However, that figure doesn't include state and local debt, "agency debt" or unfunded liabilities of entitlement programs like Social Security and Medicare.

GO BiG--Believe God for Debt Cancellation!

That figure also doesn't include personal debt, which is of primary interest to us here. According to a recent CNBC news story, outstanding credit card debt in the United States is projected to total $900 billion by the end of 2015, which means the average family's household debt is $7,813. Can you relate?

The Creditors Are Coming, the Creditors Are Coming!

During the time of Elisha, the widow of a prophet could certainly relate. Once her husband was dead and her protective covering was gone, the creditors began to hound her for money she didn't have. Unless she paid her debt, she would lose her sons to servitude, in order to pay off their creditors. She could have lost her home and become a beggar. That's no way for a prophet's wife to end up – or anyone else, for that matter!

Debt Is No Joke

I'll ask the question again: Can you relate? Comedians make jokes about parents who refuse to answer the telephone because they're ducking creditors, or their children tell debt collectors, "She said to tell you she's not home!" We laugh at those jokes, but anyone who has "been there, done that" will tell you the weight of debt is no laughing matter.

Many of you reading this book either have faced or are facing the loss of your home to foreclosure, repossession of your automobile, or bankruptcy. And let's not talk about student loan debt. Lord help us!

GO BiG--Believe God for Debt Cancellation!

Where to Turn?

The widow knew exactly where to go – she looked to the man of God for wisdom. She didn't waste time wallowing in self-pity and grief; she knew she needed to GO BiG! She got up and sought help for her dilemma. She put her faith in action, and believed Elisha would give her a word from the Lord to address her situation.

Notice that Elisha didn't give the widow a handout; he first asked her what she had on hand. She told him all she had was a jar of oil, but we know that "little becomes much" when it's placed in God's capable hands. I'm reminded of the young boy in John 6:1-14 who had a sack lunch of five little loaves and two fish. When Jesus asked Phillip what they could do to feed the multitude, he expressed doubt and a lack of faith. Contemplating the challenge of feeding thousands of hungry men, not including women and children, Phillip said to Jesus, "Two hundred pennyworth of bread is not sufficient for them, that every one of them may take a little."

Andrew's answer was just as doubtful. He knew what was available and had seen the miracles Jesus had done in the past, yet he too failed to respond in faith. After giving it some thought he mentioned what they had on hand: "There is a lad here, which hath five barley loaves, and two small fishes: but what are they among so many?" Phillip and Andrew each had an opportunity to GO BiG in their thinking, but they apparently forgot they were in the presence of the King of kings for whom nothing is impossible.

There Is a Word – And A Plan of Action – From the Lord

Jesus gave the disciples a plan of action: First make the men sit down. After blessing the bread and fish, the lunch was multiplied

GO BiG--Believe God for Debt Cancellation!

to such an extent that the disciples were able to gather twelve full baskets of leftovers!

Elisha also gave the widow a plan of action. He instructed her to go and borrow as many empty jars and pots as possible from all her neighbors. Once she'd borrowed the vessels, she was to shut the door behind her and her sons, and start filling the vessels from her original pot of oil. And what did the widow do? With the freedom of her sons on the line, she decided to GO BiG!

Imagine Debt Cancellation – For Life!

We can only speculate on the number of vessels she borrowed. What we do know is that after all the borrowed vessels were filled, Elisha gave her the final steps in the plan. She was to sell the oil, pay off her debt, and get this: she and her sons were to live off the rest. The widow went so BiG that she experienced debt cancellation – for life!

Go Deeper

How would you rate your financial situation? Do you have enough faith to GO BiG and give your debt to God?

NOTES

GO BiG In LEADERSHIP!
From Coward to Champion

*And when they had kindled a fire in the midst of the hall, and were
set down together, Peter sat down among them. But a certain maid
beheld him as he sat by the fire, and earnestly looked upon him,
and said, This man was also with him. And he denied him, saying,
Woman, I know him not. And after a little while another saw him,
and said, Thou art also of them. And Peter said, Man, I am not.
And about the space of one hour after another confidently
affirmed, saying, Of a truth this fellow also was with him: for he is
a Galilaean. And Peter said, Man, I know not what thou sayest.
And immediately, while he yet spake, the cock crew.
And the Lord turned, and looked upon Peter. And Peter
remembered the word of the Lord, how he had said unto him,
Before the cock crow, thou shalt deny me thrice.
And Peter went out, and wept bitterly.*

*Then Peter said unto them, Repent,
and be baptized every one of you in the name of Jesus Christ
for the remission of sins, and ye shall receive the gift of the Holy
Ghost. For the promise is unto you, and to your children, and to all
that are afar off, even as many as the Lord our God shall call.
And with many other words did he testify and exhort, saying
Save yourselves from this untoward generation.
Then they that gladly received his word were baptized:
and the same day there were added unto them
about three thousand souls.*

Luke 22:55-62; Acts 2:36-41

Poor Peter! Big, blustery and ready to fight at the drop of a hat,
(John 18:10) his false bravado and pride often landed him in hot

GO BiG In LEADERSHIP!
From Coward to Champion

water. But we have to give Peter credit; he wasn't afraid of ghosts and he certainly wasn't afraid to step out of boats (Matthew 14:28). Just before His crucifixion Jesus had been surrounded by soldiers sent by the Chief Priests and Pharisees, when Peter pulled out his sword to protect Him. Peter was never afraid to fight--in fact–his size, confidence and boldness earned him an undisputed leadership role among the disciples.

The Original Cowardly Lion

Despite the many examples of apparent bravery, we see in his life, when we look deeper we also see something that's very disturbing – cowardice. At a very critical juncture, when faced with the choice between denying Him, or boldly proclaiming both his relationship with and allegiance to Christ, Peter wimped out. Shaken and terrified by Jesus' arrest and wondering if he was next, he used oaths and profanity to make his point, denying that He had ever known the Lord.

Shaken to the Core

It didn't take Peter long to come to grips with what he'd done. The crowing of a common barnyard animal – a rooster – reminded him of Jesus' prophetic words uttered only hours earlier: "Verily I say unto thee, that this night, before the cock crow, thou shalt deny me thrice" (Matthew 26:34). To make matters worse, Luke tells us that at the moment the cock crowed Jesus turned and looked at Peter. Needless to say, with that one look Peter was shaken to the core, realizing that not only was he a coward, he was a complete

GO BiG In LEADERSHIP!
From Coward to Champion

and utter failure. He went out and wept bitterly. How's that for leadership skills?

Leadership Lost?

I'm sure Peter thought his discipleship days were over and his relationship with Christ was a thing of the past. He had done the unthinkable, the unforgivable. How could he lead people to Christ when he couldn't even hold his own when confronted by a servant? And why would Jesus even want him anymore? After witnessing Jesus' brutal crucifixion Peter's hopes rose when he saw the empty tomb. However, after a while, his faith lapsed again. In fact, Peter actually left the ministry behind and returned to fishing for fish instead of for men. (John 21:3).

Have you experienced a failure in your ministry? Have you denied the Lord by your words or actions? Have you been caught up in sexual immorality or misconduct? Are you living in what you and God know to be hypocrisy – professing one thing at church yet living a lie elsewhere? Have you received an open rebuke because of rebellion or disobedience to those in authority over you (Hebrews 13:17)? Have you forfeited your leadership role due to your foolish actions?

God's Got a Plan

Answer this question: Where would any of us be without the mercy and goodness of the Lord? He truly looks beyond our faults and sees our needs! In Jeremiah 29:11, God sent a message to the nation of Israel in captivity: "For I know the thoughts that I think toward you, saith the LORD, thoughts of peace, and not of evil, to give you an expected end." Just as the Lord had good plans

GO BiG In LEADERSHIP!
From Coward to Champion

for Israel, He had good plans for Peter as well. Remember, He had prayed for Peter before he warned him that he would deny Him: "But I have prayed for thee, that thy faith fail not: and when thou art converted, strengthen thy brethren" (Luke 22:32).

Despite prophesying Peter's failure, Jesus had a plan and purpose for Peter's life – and He has one for you as well!

Redemption and Restoration

In addition to an angel who specifically mentioned Peter when he told the women to tell the disciples of Jesus' resurrection (Mark 16:7), Jesus also engaged in some face time with Peter when He recommissioned him (John 21:15-17). Just as he'd denied Jesus three times, Peter was three times given the opportunity to declare his love for his Savior and be recommissioned. Sweet redemption!

If you've walked away from your calling because of failure, I invite you to return to the Lord with your whole heart. Just as He promised to restore Israel after the ravages of rebellion and captivity (Jeremiah 29:14), He promises to restore it all when we repent. His gifts and callings are irrevocable and will not be withdrawn (Romans 11:29). Return to Him, and He will return to you (Malachi 3:7).

BiG Preaching

With his faith and confidence restored, Peter went on to become a preaching dynamo – winning 3,000 souls to Christ with a single passionate sermon (Acts 2:41)! Anointed by the Holy Spirit and

GO BiG In LEADERSHIP!
From Coward to Champion

filled with holy boldness, Peter assumed his God-ordained place of leadership in the New Testament church and lived out his amazing destiny.

Go Deeper

In what areas has your leadership been compromised because you're giving in to fear and cowardice? What steps can you take today to GO BiG in your ministry?

NOTES

GO BiG-- From A Fearful Weakling
to A Mighty Man

*And there came an angel of the LORD, and sat under an oak which
was in Ophrah, that pertained unto Joash the Abiezrite
and his son Gideon threshed wheat
by the winepress to hide it from the Midianites.
And the angel of the LORD appeared unto him, and said unto him,
The LORD is with thee, thou mighty man of valour. And Gideon
said unto him, Oh my Lord, if the LORD be with us, why then is all
this befallen us? And where be all his miracles which our fathers
told us of, saying, Did not the LORD bring us up from Egypt? But
now the LORD hath forsaken us, and delivered us into the hands of
the Midianites. And the LORD looked upon him, and said, Go in
this thy might, and thou shalt save Israel from the hand of the
Midianites: have not I sent thee? And he said unto him, Oh my
Lord, wherewith shall I save Israel? Behold, my family is poor in
Manasseh, and I am the least in my father's house.
And the LORD said unto him, Surely I will be with thee
and thou shalt smite the Midianites as one man.*

Judges 6:11-16

Are you anything like Gideon? Do you have a call of God on
your life, but you're too afraid to acknowledge it? Maybe you
don't come from a family of preachers, teachers or evangelists and
you believe people would question your calling. Maybe you've
experienced a troubled past and you don't feel "worthy enough" to
speak for God. Maybe you look at yourself in the mirror and think,
"Who, me?"

GO BiG-- From A Fearful Weakling
to A Mighty Man

When What You "See" Affects Your Vision

Gideon had many self-esteem issues, the first of which affected his people. The Israelites had developed a regular pattern of making promises to God and then rebelling against His leadership, which then led to captivity and eventual deliverance by a Judge, before returning to God and then once again forsaking Him- you get the picture.

Gideon's second problem? Even though Israel's disobedience had once again led to captivity, Gideon saw that Israel's sad state of affairs was actually the result of God's absence. He was hiding near a winepress while threshing out wheat, when he responded to the angel of the LORD and revealed his faulty thinking. When told that the Lord was with him and that he was a "mighty man of valor," Gideon defaulted his erroneous view of God when he asked, "If the LORD be with us, why then is all this befallen us? And where be all his miracles which our fathers told us of, saying, Did not the LORD bring us up from Egypt?"

The things Gideon "saw" filled him with such a sense of hopelessness and despair that he declared aloud what he believed: "But now the LORD hath forsaken us, and delivered us into the hands of the Midianites."

Countering Gideon's claims, the LORD was quite patient and persistent. "Go in this thy might, and thou shalt save Israel from the hand of the Midianites: have not I sent thee?"

Those last five words alone show us that Gideon knew of God's call to leadership. Gideon's resistance and statements about God were laced with fear and a corresponding lack of self-esteem – the true reasons for his failure to heed the call.

GO BiG-- From A Fearful Weakling
to A Mighty Man!

How Do You See Yourself?

Gideon's view of Israel and his thoughts about the seeming lack of God's presence reveal his third problem: His opinion of himself was just as low, or worse!

Even though the angel of the LORD had referred to him as "thou mighty man of valor," and told him that God was with him, Gideon's poor self-image got in his way. Instead of seeing himself as God saw him, Gideon looked at his life – and at his calling – through his weak and limited spiritual vision. "Oh my Lord," he said, "wherewith shall I save Israel? Behold, my family is poor in Manasseh, and I am the least in my father's house."

Answer this question: How do you see yourself? Rather than responding to God's call and seeing yourself as He sees you, in what ways do you allow fear and doubt to distort and undermine your faith? You claim to have your "reasons," but, they are nothing more than excuses, just like Gideon used. What excuses are you making?

See Yourself as God Sees You

You will not GO BiG or be successful in leadership until you see yourself as God sees you. You see the problems, the flaws, your past, the ridicule and all the reasons why you shouldn't answer the call. Despite all these things, the mere fact that God called you provides all the reasons why you should step out in obedience to that call. Shake off the shackles of fear, doubt, unbelief and low self-esteem. Put on the whole armor of God,

GO BiG-- From A Fearful Weakling
to A Mighty Man

believe what His Word says about you, and ask Him to help you see yourself through heaven's eyes. Then GO BiG in ministry!

From Weakling to Military Strategist

We know how Gideon's story ended. After asking the Lord for signs and "putting out a fleece," Gideon decided to GO BiG and rose in the strength of God to defeat the enemies of Israel. He said yes to the call of God on his life. Executing some divinely-issued, military strategies, Gideon moved into his destiny as a Deliverer and Judge.

Go Deeper

When will you stop making excuses and stop allowing fear to prevent you from saying yes to God's call to leadership? What steps will you take today to move forth in the ministry you know God has called you to do?

NOTES

GO BiG--Handle Your Business!

She considereth a field, and buyeth it:
with the fruit of her hands she planteth a vineyard.
She girdeth her loins with strength, and strengtheneth her arms.
She perceiveth that her merchandise is good: her candle goeth not
out by night. She maketh fine linen, and selleth it; and delivereth
girdles unto the merchant. Favour is deceitful, and beauty is vain:
but a woman that feareth the Lord, she shall be praised.
Give her of the fruit of her hands;
and let her own works praise her in the gates.

Proverbs 31:16-18, 24; 30-31

And on the sabbath we went out of the city by a river side, where
prayer was wont to be made; and we sat down, and spake unto the
women which resorted thither. And a certain woman named Lydia,
a seller of purple, of the city of Thyatira, which worshipped God,
heard us: whose heart the Lord opened, that she attended unto the
things which were spoken of Paul. And when she was baptized,
and her household, she besought us, saying,
If ye have judged me to be faithful to the Lord,
come into my house, and abide there
And she constrained us.

Acts 16:13-15

Deborah, as mentioned earlier, was in an unusual position, as women in that day were unlikely to be placed in positions of power and authority. Also noted previously is that just as in the case of Deborah, God often chooses to do the exact opposite of what is expected; raising up ordinary people and causing them to stand out from the masses to do extraordinary things.

GO BiG--Handle Your Business!

The same is true of two other women also mentioned in the Bible. The Proverbs 31 woman and Lydia of Thyatira come to mind, when contemplating the notion of successful women in business. In fact, they are excellent models for us to emulate. They were organized high achievers, diligent to invest long hours of hard work to meet the needs of their families.

Taking Care of Business

The Proverbs 31 woman was married, and she was active in several business ventures. When we read her story, we discover that she made and sold various kinds of needlework and tapestries done in a wide number of mediums. She also bought and sold real estate, planted and operated a vineyard, and was the equivalent of a modern-day clothier and tailor. She earned the trust of her husband's early on. So much so that he didn't worry when she was in and out, going about her business. He and their children were proud of her accomplishments and held her in high esteem!

This woman was no slouch as she was involved in a vast number of activities. In addition to managing several different income streams, she made sure that the members of her household--including her servants – were well-nourished and well-dressed. The productivity of this woman was incredible. There was nothing lazy about her. Though her schedule was probably busy and hectic, she not once uttered a complaint. She was busy taking care of business.

We don't know quite as much about Lydia as we do the woman in Proverbs 31. Lydia was "a seller of purple," which means she sold and possibly made purple dye. She was a merchant, so she

GO BiG--Handle Your Business!

owned her own business. Lydia holds the distinction of being the first Christian convert on the European continent!

The fact that she had "a household" indicates that she was a woman of means. Scripture mentions no husband, and some theologians believe she was a widow. Whether she never married or was widowed, Lydia was self-supporting and consequently earned the respect of the city, so much so that she could freely invite the Apostle Paul and others into her home.

When Your Life Is a Witness for God

The lives of both Lydia and the Proverbs 31 woman serve as a powerful witness for God. The Proverbs 31 woman exemplified martial fidelity as well as the diligent, loving care of her children. All too often, even Christian men and women permit outside influences to slowly assume more importance than they should, resulting in the gradual erosion of their marriages and family relationships. Unfortunately, they climb the career ladder, allowing the accumulation of money, power or success, to become their gods and often at the expense of those they claim to love. And while it's true that we must earn a living it should not become the focus, so that our families are left behind. To that end, we must make sure our priorities line up with Scripture—that is, putting God first, and after that, family and self.

As a single woman, Lydia enjoyed a bit more flexibility. However, the story of her conversion shows her spiritual mindset and dedication to the things of God. When Paul and his party entered the city to share the gospel and went to a regularly-scheduled prayer meeting held near a river, Lydia was there. Scripture tells us that Lydia "worshipped God," and her heart was open to hear, receive and believe on the Lord Jesus Christ. In

GO BiG--Handle Your Business!

addition to holding the distinction as the first convert in Europe, theologians also believe Lydia's home served as the meeting place for the Philippian church.

GO BiG in Entrepreneurship

According to the "2015 State of Women-Owned Businesses Report" commissioned by American Express Open, the number of women-owned businesses grew by 74% between 1997 and 2015. This rate is 1.5 times the national average. In fact, women now own 30% of all businesses in the United States. And interestingly enough, black business women compose the fastest-growing group of entrepreneurs in America!

In light of this information, there's never been a better time than now for anyone – especially women – to GO BiG in entrepreneurship! Do you dream of being the CEO of your own company and directing the trajectory of your career and personal accomplishments? Think about it. If Lydia and the Proverbs 31 woman could believe God, flex their entrepreneurial muscles, and excel in business and leadership in a time when women had very little autonomy, what's hindering you from being able to GO BiG?

Go Deeper

What steps are you taking to realize your dreams of entrepreneurship? In what areas of your life do you need to "handle your business" to move forward in reaching your goals?

NOTES

GO BiG--Age Is Just a Number

Let no man despise thy youth; but be thou an example of the believers, in word, in conversation, in charity, in spirit, in faith, in purity. Till I come, give attendance to reading, to exhortation, to doctrine. Neglect not the gift that is in thee, which was given thee by prophecy, with the laying on of the hands of the presbytery.

1 Timothy 4:12-14

Do you believe the old saying, "Age is just a number?" I'll tell you something that isn't a secret: God does. How do I know? He uses whomever He wills – regardless of their age.

Multicultural Background and Spiritual Foundation

In Scripture, we discover that Timothy's family background was multicultural, similar to many homes today. Timothy himself was biracial; his father was Greek and his mother, Eunice was a Jewess who spoke fluent Greek. Though he wasn't circumcised as an infant, Timothy was raised to know his Jewish heritage. His mother Eunice and grandmother, Lois were converted to the Christian faith during Paul's first missionary journey to Derbe and Lystra and were commended for their "unfeigned faith" (2 Timothy 1:5).

Timothy became a young convert under the ministry of the Apostle Paul, who loved him dearly and referred to him as "my beloved son" (1 Corinthians 4:17), "my own son in the faith" (1 Timothy 1:2) and "my dearly beloved son." As Timothy's father in the faith Paul allowed him to work closely with him in ministry. Paul also served as his mentor and later laid hands on him and ordained him as a pastor (2 Timothy 1:6).

GO BiG--Age Is Just a Number

You're Never Too Young to GO BiG

We usually associate young people with exuberance, a zest for life and an abundance of energy. In fact, older adults often feel the need to rein them in and slow them down for one reason or another. Youth are sometimes overlooked or worse, considered too young, inexperienced and therefore "not ready" to be used of God.

Unfortunately, constant, unrelenting hindrance can adversely affect a young person's spiritual growth so that even a go-getter becomes timid and insecure, refusing to speak up even when he has something valid to add to the conversation. Others are intimidated in the presence of mature saints with more poise and experience. And let's face it. Instead of offering wisdom and encouragement some older believers, by words or behavior, reinforce the old adage that young people "should be seen and not heard." When this happens the church suffers, as it forfeits the benefits that every member brings to the body (1 Corinthians 12:14-23).

You're Not Too Young to GO BiG

For someone who lived hundreds of years ago, the Apostle Paul was very progressive in his thoughts and actions! He recognized that Timothy was easily intimidated and was retreating instead of moving forward. Thankfully, Paul encouraged him, saying, "Let no man despise thy youth; but be thou an example of the believers, in word, in conversation, in charity, in spirit, in faith, in purity" (1 Timothy 4:12).

GO BiG--Age Is Just a Number

Wait, what? Paul said what? He let Timothy know that he should not allow anyone to prevent him from living up to his God-given potential, but should offer his life as an example for others to follow. In essence, Paul was saying, "Timothy, you're not too young to GO BiG!"

Go For It!

So, which group do you fall into? Do you belong to what is popularly referred to as Generation Z, those born between the years 1995 and 2012? Or are you a Millennial, born between 1977 and 1994? If you are, I encourage you to take to heart the words of the Apostle Paul, and even commit them to memory. Don't let anyone despise or belittle you for being young. Now, this doesn't mean you should be arrogant or overbearing. Follow Timothy's example and partner with a mature Christian who can mentor you in the ways of God. Take heed to wise counsel, and be a shining example of what it means to be saved and on fire for the Lord.

In the kingdom of heaven, age really is just a number. Young person, it's your time to GO BiG in God!

Go Deeper

Take a close look at the members of your church. Prayerfully ask the Lord for a godly adult who can mentor and guide your spiritual life in the same way that Paul helped Timothy.

NOTES

You Can Be the Wing Man –
and You Can Still GO BiG

And it came to pass, when he had made an end of speaking unto
Saul, that the soul of Jonathan was knit with the soul of David,
and Jonathan loved him as his own soul.
And Saul took him that day,
and would let him go no more home to his father's house.
Then Jonathan and David made a covenant
because he loved him as his own soul.
And Jonathan stripped himself of the robe that was upon him, and
gave it to David, and his garments, even to his sword, and to his
bow, and to his girdle. And David saw that Saul was come out to
seek his life: and David was in the wilderness of Ziph in a wood.
And Jonathan Saul's son arose, and went to David into the wood,
and strengthened his hand in God. And he said unto him, Fear not:
for the hand of Saul my father shall not find thee; and thou shalt be
king over Israel, and I shall be next unto thee
and that also Saul my father knoweth.
1 Samuel 18:1-4; 23:15-17

In a previous chapter we discussed the importance of "ride or die" friends. You know, those friends who would go with you to the ends of the earth and back. The paralyzed man whose four friends carried him to Jesus was blessed to have "ride or die" friends. But did you know that there's another kind of friend that's just as important? A wing man.

Everybody Needs a Wing Man

The modern day meaning of the term "wing man" refers to a man who accompanies a friend, offering moral support when his friend approaches a potential romantic partner. Most people use the

You Can Be the Wing Man –
and You Can Still GO BiG

term with that meaning in mind, yet most people don't know that the term "wing man" originated in the aeronautics industry. When planes fly in formation, the wing man's plane is located behind and slightly to the side of the lead aircraft. The wing man isn't the lead. His role is that of support. Why is the wing man important? He's there to give aid and backup if the lead pilot runs into trouble.

Yes, it's important to have a friend or friends who fit the "ride or die" category. Nevertheless, at times you may experience a situation when you need a wing man. In Scripture we discover that David reached that place in his life – and his beloved friend, Jonathan stepped up to be the perfect wing man.

Recognizing Your Role and Knowing Your Place

A wing man is successful because he recognizes his role and he knows his place. He understands his role is secondary to that of the lead man and his place is behind and beside him, not in front. As King Saul's heir apparent, Jonathan was next in line for the throne. And yet, he recognized that he was not destined to be king. More importantly, he accepted that fact with grace. Jonathan knew his place was not in front of David, but behind and beside him, doing whatever he could to promote David to the place for which God had destined him—the throne.

Get this: Jonathan embraced the role of wing man knowing full well that his father hated David and wanted him dead. Saul was living in rebellion and opposition to God's clearly revealed will, yet Jonathan embraced the will of God and sought to do what he could to bring it to pass. More than anything, Jonathan knew his role and his place was to obey God.

You Can Be the Wing Man –
and You Can Still GO BiG

A Different Kind of Leadership

Read the story of David and Jonathan, and you'll also discover Jonathan's natural leadership ability. He led troops of men and won battles, and stood up to his father on behalf of David and the nation of Israel. Secure and confident in his identity, he fulfilled his God-given destiny.

Are you an Assistant or Associate Pastor? Maybe a First Assistant to a Bishop or national department leader? Are you an Assistant to the head of a women's ministry; a co-chair or vice president?

In other words, do you hold a position that others deem "second fiddle?" If so, don't despair and for goodness' sake, don't be embarrassed or ashamed of the vital contribution you make from right where you are.

Jonathan excelled in the realm of leadership, and as wing man to David, he provided a different kind of leadership. You see, it takes strength of leadership to point men away from you and toward someone else.

God-Given and Rare

If you have good leadership skills, yet (1) can recognize the hand of God on someone else as the leader, and (2) understand that God wants you to support and promote that person, then you exemplify a different kind of leadership that is God-given – and rare.

It's rare because society teaches us to "look out for Number One," and unfortunately, that spirit has crept into the church. It takes a special man – and a special kind of leader – to walk in his role as wing man to the Lord's designated leader. It takes a special

You Can Be the Wing Man –
and You Can Still GO BiG

man to be a true confidante and to engage in the ministry of support. Consider Joshua and Moses, Elisha and Elijah and Paul and Silas, to name a few.

If you're the wing man, continue to appreciate your leadership role in the body of Christ. GO BiG in your support of God's chosen leader, and let Him use you for His glory!

Go Deeper

What can you do in your role as wing man to lift up your leader – and shine for God – even more?

NOTES

GO BiG--For the Right Reasons

But there was a certain man, called Simon,
which before time in the same city used sorcery,
and bewitched the people of Samaria,
giving out that himself was some great one:
To whom they all gave heed, from the least to the greatest, saying,
this man is the great power of God. And to him they had regard,
because that of long time he had bewitched them with sorceries.
But when they believed Philip preaching the things concerning the
kingdom of God, and the name of Jesus Christ, they were baptized,
both men and women. Then Simon himself believed also: and when
he was baptized, he continued with Philip, and wondered,
beholding the miracles and signs which were done. And when
Simon saw that through laying on of the apostles' hands the Holy
Ghost was given, he offered them money, Saying,
give me also this power, that on whomsoever I lay hands,
he may receive the Holy Ghost. But Peter said unto him,
Thy money perish with thee,
because thou hast thought that the gift of God
may be purchased with money.
Thou hast neither part nor lot in this matter
for thy heart is not right in the sight of God.

Acts 8:9-13, 18-21

We've all seen them: the people who are seemingly fascinated by the church. They love the great music and singing, the anointed preaching and teaching, the fervor and passion of the evangelistic services, and the excitement of services filled with shouting and dancing. They love church and demonstrate it by attending every revival that comes to town as well as all the national convocations and conferences, and of course, local meetings. They know church

GO BiG--For the Right Reasons

– but they don't know Jesus. I'll go you one better. Sometimes, these people are church leaders.

False Leadership

Simon the Sorcerer was one such person. Prior to the arrival of Paul and the other Apostles, Simon was seen and respected as an anointed spiritual leader. They didn't know he was using sorcery and witchcraft instead of the true power of the Holy Spirit. Simon didn't point people to God; he pointed them to himself. Instead of encouraging people to glorify God, Simon encouraged people to glorify him.

Regardless of whom it comes from, know that leadership that points people away from God and to a human personality is not true scriptural leadership.

Simon's hold on his town was broken when some truly anointed apostles and disciples came to town. They each had a deep, personal relationship with God, and the signs and wonders and miracles they displayed were   empowered by the Holy Spirit. In fact, people began to get saved and to recognize the true and living God when they saw Him, only to realize it was far different from the sham Simon offered them.

False Christians

Many saints who strive to live lives pleasing to God are deeply disturbed by the sights and sounds they see in church. They are troubled by the number of high-profile, headline-generating scandals that bring rebuke and scorn on those who name the name of Christ in spirit and in truth. When such scandals rock the

GO BiG--For the Right Reasons

church, saints must deal with the verbal and digital blows from those who, whether in person or on social media, gleefully proclaim, "Those church people are all a bunch of hypocrites!"

And it doesn't stop there! When egregious lifestyles are condemned by preachers of righteousness, and when Christians speak out against sin, they're accused of being judgmental and unloving. Yes, Romans 3:23 informs us that "All have sinned and come short of the glory of God." We are to speak the truth in love (Ephesians 4:15) not in condemnation or with a critical spirit that overlooks our own faults and shortcomings (Matthew 7:3-5). When we move to lift the fallen, those who are spiritual are admonished to "restore such an one in the spirit of meekness; considering thyself, lest thou also be tempted" (Galatians 6:1).

Yet, we know that we are not to turn the grace of God into lascivious, dishonorable lifestyles that give us a license to sin – God forbid! (Romans 6:15; Jude 1:4). God's Word is clear and unequivocal when dealing with issues of sin and the need to be holy, making no excuses for behaviors that disqualify us from leading God's people. The Apostle Paul includes a laundry list in 1 Corinthians 6:9-10: "Know ye not that the unrighteous shall not inherit the kingdom of God? Be not deceived: neither fornicators, nor idolaters, nor adulterers, nor effeminate, nor abusers of themselves with mankind, Nor thieves, nor covetous, nor drunkards, nor revilers, nor extortioners, shall inherit the kingdom of God."

Ain't Nothing Like the Real Thing

There's nothing like the real thing – and there is no evidence more real that when someone repents and turns from their wicked ways to serve God! Following the list of qualities that will

GO BiG--For the Right Reasons

disqualify people from heaven, Paul goes on to describe those who will be there, once real change takes place: "And such were some of you: but ye are washed, but ye are sanctified, but ye are justified in the name of the Lord Jesus, and by the Spirit of our God."

Have you been disturbed by false leaders, hypocrites and those living blatantly sinful lifestyles? Don't be. "The foundation of God standeth sure, having this seal, The Lord knoweth them that are his" (2 Timothy 2:19).

They Want What We Have

When he realized his number was up and followers were leaving in droves, Simon decided: "If you can't beat them, join them." He professed Christ and was baptized, and then started following the disciples around.

Perhaps you're wondering why the church seems to be overrun with false leaders and members with their own agendas. That's simple. They want what we have, but they don't want to pay what it costs – in surrender to God. Simon is clear proof of that. When he saw the power of God falling and people being filled with the Holy Spirit when the apostles laid hands on them, he wanted what the apostles had. He wanted the power of God and to remain in leadership, but he wanted it for all the wrong reasons. Thinking he could purchase the gifting and anointing of God with money, he offered to pay the apostles to get what they had. In the end, however, he found out just how wrong he was when he was rebuked by Peter and judged by God.

GO BiG--For the Right Reasons

He Has to Know YOU

Are you someone who loves to see the power of God demonstrated? Do you enjoy attending Spirit-filled services and desire to take an active role in leading the church? Maybe you're already leading, yet in your heart of hearts you know your relationship with Christ isn't genuine. There's nothing wrong with wanting to be used by God and to GO BiG for Him, but the desire to lead must be backed up by the right attitudes and motives. The service God accepts only comes by HIS Spirit. The ability to GO BiG is only available through the power of GOD.

If you're serving in the church under false pretenses and yet experiencing what you believe to be is a move of God, don't be fooled! Jesus said, "Not every one that saith unto me, Lord, Lord, shall enter into the kingdom of heaven; but he that doeth the will of my Father which is in heaven. Many will say to me in that day, Lord, Lord, have we not prophesied in thy name? and in thy name have cast out devils? and in thy name done many wonderful works? And then will I profess unto them, I never knew you: depart from me, ye that work iniquity" (Matthew 7: 21-23).

Simon the Sorcerer "believed," and yet by his actions the true light was shined on his heart. It's not enough to say you know Christ. He has to know YOU.

Go Deeper

Is your relationship with God based on a humble repentant attitude and a teachable heart? Are you in leadership for the right reasons?

NOTES

GO BiG – Busy as A Bee for God!

And Deborah, a prophetess, the wife of Lapidoth,
she judged Israel at that time.
And she dwelt under the palm tree of Deborah between Ramah and
Bethel in mount Ephraim: and the children of Israel came up to
her for judgment. And she sent and called Barak the son of
Abinoam out of Kedeshnaphtali, and said unto him, Hath not the
LORD God of Israel commanded, saying, Go and draw toward
mount Tabor, and take with thee ten thousand men of the children
of Naphtali and of the children of Zebulun? And I will draw unto
thee to the river Kishon Sisera, the captain of Jabin's army, with
his chariots and his multitude; and I will deliver him into thine
hand. And Barak said unto her, If thou wilt go with me, then I will
go: but if thou wilt not go with me, then I will not go. And she said,
I will surely go with thee: notwithstanding the journey that thou
takest shall not be for thine honour;
for the LORD shall sell Sisera into the hand of a woman.
And Deborah arose, and went with Barak to Kedesh. Then sang
Deborah and Barak the son of Abinoam on that day, saying, Praise
ye the LORD for the avenging * of Israel, when the people
willingly offered themselves. Hear, O ye kings; give ear,
O ye princes; I, even I, will sing unto the LORD
I will sing praise to the LORD God of Israel.

Judges 4:4-9; 5:1-3

Margaret Thatcher, the former Prime Minister of England is credited with saying, "If you want something said, ask a man; if you want something done, ask a woman."

Such was the case with the Prophetess Deborah, who served as a Judge of Israel for forty years. Israel fell away from God and became bound in captivity to Jabin king of Canaan, a man the

GO BiG – Busy as A Bee for God!

Bible describes as one who "mightily oppressed the children of Israel" (Judges 4:3). Sisera was the captain of his army, and together these two men wrought havoc on God's people.

In typical fashion, Israel cried out to the Lord for deliverance. As the loving Father He is, God heard their cries and again sent them a Judge and Deliverer.

But this time, He sent a woman. Multi-faceted In Ministry Wife. Mother in Israel. Judge. Prophetess. Poet. Warrior. Singer.

These were just a few of the titles and corresponding areas of ministry where Deborah served. In the intellectual hierarchy of the animal kingdom, bees rank high. Small wonder the name Deborah means, "bee!" Dynamic, charismatic, multi-faceted and multi-talented, the book of Judges Chapters 4-5 paint a picture of a woman greatly used by God in a number of capacities. Instead of asking, "What gifts did she possess", we might ask "What gifts did she not possess?"

First Corinthians Chapter 12 describes many spiritual gifts, and tells us that these gifts are distributed by the Spirit "severally as he will" (v.11). In the case of Deborah, the Holy Spirit was extremely generous. When we study her life and ministry, we see that she was ready, willing and able to GO BiG when using every single one of her gifts!

Recognizing Headship and Authority

We can't study the life of Deborah and not admit that she obviously understood the principles of headship and authority. We know this because she was highly esteemed by the men in her life and her gifts were remarkably effective.

GO BiG – Busy as A Bee for God!

Deborah was the wife of Lapidoth, whose name means "torches" or "lightning flashes." We know very little about him, yet we know a great deal concerning the social structure of Hebrew life and patricidal authority. In those ancient times, women were largely seen as little more than the property of their fathers, husbands or brothers. Deborah could not have held her position of leadership as a judge in Israel without the sanction of her husband AND of the other men in the nation.

Calm and Confident

Because she was a Prophetess, Deborah understood the will and mind of God concerning His military strategy to liberate Israel from the hands of Jabin and Sisera. She knew what God wanted done, and she also knew that Barak, captain of the armies of Israel, was also aware of God's will. And yet, Barack had not moved to make it happen.

Unlike Barak – the head of Israel's army, no less – Deborah refused to shy away from her leadership responsibilities. She understood an elementary, yet pivotal component of leadership: timely obedience to God's revealed and stated will.

Calmly and confidently, and in no way attempting to shame the man of God, she sent for Barak. She said unto him, "Hath not the LORD God of Israel commanded, saying, Go and draw toward mount Tabor, and take with thee ten thousand men of the children of Naphtali and of the children of Zebulun? And I will draw unto thee to the river Kishon Sisera, the captain of Jabin's army, with his chariots and his multitude; and I will deliver him into thine hand" (Judges 4:6-7).

GO BiG – Busy as A Bee for God!

When you truly possess the ministry, and calling of a prophetess, you are unafraid to reveal God's message. You will move in confidence – and you will also move in wisdom, seeking to preserve the honor and dignity of those to whom you speak. Quietness and confidence is your strength (Isaiah 30:15) – not arrogance, clamor, confusion or bluster.

Bold and Fearless

Acknowledging the truth of Deborah's words, Barak agreed to obey God and go after Sisera. He put forth one caveat: he would only go if she went with him! Needless to say, that was a highly unusual request, because women didn't go into battle with men. Barak's request reflects an incredible level of confidence in her and reveals his need for her support. Bold and fearless, Deborah agreed to go with Barak to the battle. She didn't berate or emasculate him; she simply informed him that the credit for the battle would go to an unlikely person – a woman.

Walking in Wisdom

Clearly, the hand of the Lord was upon her, and she was God's chosen leader for her time. Her divine appointment was apparent, acknowledged and accepted.

Are you a multi-faceted, multi-talented woman who is gifted by God to operate in different capacities? Then be sure to follow in the footsteps of Deborah. Know and understand that when the hand of the Lord is over your life and His anointing rests upon you, there is no need to usurp authority or demand recognition. Your

GO BiG – Busy as A Bee for God!

gift and your anointing will make room for you (Proverbs 18:16). It is God's responsibility, not yours, to make room and a place for you and your ministry. He is the One who opens doors no man can shut (Revelation 3:8).

Displaying the wisdom that is a hallmark of anointed women, Deborah did not attempt to become the King of Israel. Instead, note how she describes her spiritual ascent in Judges 5:7: "The inhabitants of the villages ceased, they ceased in Israel, until that I Deborah arose, that I arose a mother in Israel."

She didn't point to her spiritual gifts, or her position as a Judge and Deliverer. Instead, she described herself as a mother in Israel, someone who nurtures, sustains and loves. She walked in wisdom, knew who and what she was in God, and judged Israel for forty years.

Go Deeper

Think about the way you use your gifts and operate within your ministry. Do you walk in wisdom, quietness and confidence? Are you bold and fearless, yet respectful? In what areas of life and ministry do you need to trust God more and rely upon yourself less?

NOTES

GO BiG--Even When Your Time
Is Out of Season!

For I delivered unto you first of all that which I also received, how that Christ died for our sins according to the scriptures; And that he was buried, and that he rose again the third day according to the scriptures: And that he was seen of Cephas, then of the twelve: After that, he was seen of above five hundred brethren at once; of whom the greater part remain unto this present, but some are fallen asleep. After that, he was seen of James; then of all the apostles. And last of all he was seen of me also, as of one born out of due time. For I am the least of the apostles, that am not meet to be called an apostle, because I persecuted the church of God. But by the grace of God I am what I am: and his grace which was bestowed upon me was not in vain; but I laboured more abundantly than they all: yet not I,
but the grace of God which was with me.

1 Corinthians 15:3-10

Sharing his testimony in Philippians 3:4-5, the Apostle Paul said this, "Though I might also have confidence in the flesh. If any other man thinketh that he hath whereof he might trust in the flesh, I more: circumcised the eighth day, of the stock of Israel, of the tribe of Benjamin, an Hebrew of the Hebrews; as touching the law, a Pharisee; Concerning zeal, persecuting the church; touching the righteousness which is in the law, blameless."

Those were impressive credentials any Hebrew could be proud of. And yet, this mighty man of God viewed his face-to-face meeting with Jesus and subsequent calling to the ministry "as of one born out of due time."

So how can you GO BiG in leadership when you know you're born out of season? The Apostle Paul shows us how.

GO BiG--Even When Your Time
Is Out of Season!

Get Over Yourself

Paul could GO BiG in ministry because he was willing to get over himself. In His infinite wisdom and design, the Lord helped Paul get over himself at their first meeting. After aiding and commending those who stoned Stephen (Acts 8:1) Paul was ready to do even more. He moved forward with his plan to eradicate Christianity, and wasted no time receiving permission and credentials from the High Priest to go out and arrest those who named the name of Christ. Filled with self-righteous, pharisaic pride and outrage at what he considered blasphemy, Paul thought he was doing God a favor.

Well, in Acts 9, we see that God showed him otherwise! He gave Paul a knockout punch to beat all knockout punches; the overwhelming power and presence of the resurrected Christ knocked Paul down to the ground – both literally and figuratively. Imagine this high and mighty Pharisee scrambling around in the dirt, blind and trembling! When he was told to stop "kicking against the pricks" Paul was further humiliated by being told to go into the city and await further instructions.

If you're counting on your education, secular credentials or even your spiritual lineage to give you a leg up on everyone else, think again. Yes, God can use your inherent and learned talents and abilities. He did this with Paul, with Moses, who was "learned in all the wisdom of the Egyptians, and was mighty in words and in deeds" (Acts 7:22). Daniel was another intellectually-gifted Bible character, "in whom was no blemish, but well favored, and skillful in all wisdom, and cunning in knowledge, and understanding science" (Daniel 1:4).

GO BiG--Even When Your Time Is Out of Season!

God used these and other "educated" people, yet unlike the world, He certainly wasn't and is still not impressed by them and isn't limited when He chooses who to use for His glory. So when you're tempted to be full of yourself, remember the words Paul wrote in 1 Corinthians 1:26-29: "For ye see your calling, brethren, how that not many wise men after the flesh, not many mighty, not many noble, are called: But God hath chosen the foolish things of the world to confound the wise; and God hath chosen the weak things of the world to confound the things which are mighty; And base things of the world, and things which are despised, hath God chosen, yea, and things which are not, to bring to nought things that are: That no flesh should glory in his presence."

Put away your pride and sense of self-importance, and consider the reaction of the religious leaders who tried to persecute the apostles: "Now when they saw the boldness of Peter and John, and perceived that they were unlearned and ignorant men, they marvelled; and they took knowledge of them, that they had been with Jesus" (Acts 4:13).

If you want to GO BiG in God, the important thing is to get over yourself, and instead live so that people take note of the fact that you've been with Jesus.

Recognize the Importance of the Message-And the Calling.

Once he was converted and got over himself, Paul became a fool for Christ (1 Corinthians 4:10), passionate about sharing the good news of Jesus Christ. The message was simple: Christ died for our sins according to the scriptures; he was buried, and he rose again the third day according to the scriptures. Paul knew that the truth of the message of Christ's death, burial and resurrection was more important than any other message, because if it was a lie, we

GO BiG--Even When Your Time
Is Out of Season!

are completely and utterly dead in our sins, lost, and forever separated from God. Hallelujah! The message is true, and we are assured the victory through our Lord Jesus Christ.

Paul also recognized the importance of his calling – so much so he not only staked his life on it, he shaped his entire life around it. He wasn't happy unless he was preaching, teaching, witnessing and winning souls to Christ. Paul felt compelled to preach the gospel, and shows us in 1 Corinthians 9:16 that he considered preaching the very least he could do for God: "For though I preach the gospel, I have nothing to glory of: for necessity is laid upon me; yea, woe is unto me, if I preach not the gospel!"

It's easy to GO BiG when you recognize the importance of the message, and you're committed to your calling instead of to yourself!

Keep Pressing Forward

And last, but not least, Paul was able to GO BiG even when he felt out of season because he continued to press forward. From those within the church Paul endured the ridicule of his presence and speech (2 Corinthians 10:10) and questions about his worthiness and standing as an apostle (1 Corinthians 9). From those outside the church, Paul experienced severe persecution (2 Corinthians 11:23-28) and eventual martyrdom (2 Timothy 4:6-8).

Despite all these things, from the time of his conversion and his fateful meeting with Jesus on the road to Damascus, Paul's life and ministry was marked by a GO BiG mindset. He refused to give in and he absolutely would not give up! Instead, with his focus on Christ, he testified, "This one thing I do, forgetting those things

GO BiG--Even When Your Time
Is Out of Season!

which are behind, and reaching forth unto those things which are before, I press toward the mark for the prize of the high calling of God in Christ Jesus" (Philippians 3:13-14).

Want to GO BiG in ministry and leadership regardless of the season? Get over yourself, recognizing the importance of the Message and the calling, and keep pressing forward!

Go Deeper

What steps do you need to take to get over yourself? In what ways do you demonstrate your understanding of the importance of the gospel message and the leadership and ministry call God has placed on your life? In what areas of your life do you need to keep pressing forward?

NOTES

1. Protection – Rahab
2. Enlarged Territory – Jabez
3. Abundance – Disciples in boat
4. Debt cancellation – Widow who obeyed Elijah
5. Healing – Woman with issue of blood
6. Deliverance – Man in the tombs
7. Rewards of Intercession – 4 friends and man with palsy
8. The Centurion – You don't have to see it to believe it!

Leadership
1. Peter – initial cowardice/compromise to strong leadership
2. Gideon – Low self-esteem to confident military strategist
3. Jonathan – willing to be the wing man
4. Deborah
5. Lydia
6. Barnabus – the charismatic leader (style AND substance)
7. Paul – Leader seemingly born out of season
8. Elijah
9. Moses
10. Simon the sorcerer